Translated from the French by Harriet Mason

First published in Great Britain in 1998
by Thames and Hudson Ltd, London

British Library Cataloguing-in-Publication Data
A catalogue record for this book is available from the British Library

ISBN 0-500-018464

Printed and bound in Italy

Fortuny

Delphine Desveaux

Thames and Hudson

t he name Fortuny is so closely linked with Venice that it has entered the Venetian language, though his full name, Fortuny y Madrazo, reveals its Spanish origin.

Fortuny's Catalan grandfather was a puppet-master who made and dressed his own marionettes, but the story of this famous family of artists really began with Mariano Fortuny y Marsal, the famous couturier's father. He was a successful Spanish painter and was just beginning to be known throughout Europe when he died of malaria at the age of thirty-eight in 1874. From 1859 onwards he had been a keen orientalist – as official artist to the city of Barcelona, he was attached to General Prim's military campaigns in North Africa against the Angheran tribes, who were making incursions on Spanish colonial territory. He fell in love with Morocco – then under the governorship of Abd el Rahman – with its arts, its people and their way of life. When he went back to Spain, in his imagination he returned constantly to the world which inspired many of his oriental paintings.

Mariano Fortuny y Madrazo was born in Granada on 11 May 1871. His mother, Cecilia de Madrazo, was an imperious

Spanish beauty, whose family's wealth had endowed the Prado Museum in Madrid. Fortuny quickly gained his father's passion for painting, sculpture, design, prints, and a highly individual, Balzacian obsession with collecting. He was the last in line of one of Spain's great families, and with his rapidly acquired artistic education seemed destined to be a painter, claiming to be 'first and foremost a painter', as some are destined for the Church. However, posterity decided otherwise: his outstandingly creative work with textiles revealed that he was also a couturier, and a specifically Venetian couturier.

n owadays Fortuny is referred to as 'the magician' in the Sérénissima's newspapers; he is a curiosity – one of many that Venetians like to protect by keeping to themselves – and one of Venice's last great characters. He produced both easel paintings and monumental frescoes, and was an unsurpassed copyist, like his father, as well as a print-maker and sculptor. He was also a set designer, inventing new reflected-lighting systems, a photographer (more than ten thousand negatives are stored in the Fortuny Museum in Venice), and a collector. He designed his own furniture, as well as sometimes playing the role of antiquarian and investing in grand seventeenth-century pieces. It was only after devoting himself to each of these different fields that he turned to couture. At the age of forty, he threw himself into fashion design, like a painter trying out a new colour; for this master of so many skills, designing clothes was just another facet of his work.

The thin pleated silk dress which made his name in the twenties has echoes in the work of modern designers, from Issey

Miyake to Irena Gregori, via Krizia, Alberta Ferretti and Romeo Gigli. Fortuny's work has lived on, showing that the ephemeral has the power to endure.

Fortuny's early childhood was divided between Rome, where his father had a studio near the Via Appia, and Capricio, near Naples. After his father's death in 1874 Cecilia and the two children, Maria-Luisa, aged five, and Mariano, aged three, left for Paris to join their maternal uncle, also a painter. Fortuny studied painting until the age of eighteen, and was introduced to Parisian society and the refinements of feminine elegance, as he moved between the drawing-rooms of his uncle Raimundo's clients and his mother's, crowded with members of the Spanish artistic community. He grew up with his cousin Federico de Madrazo, known as Coco, who later became one of Proust's closest friends and also knew Cocteau; he was involved in drafting the libretto for *Le Dieu bleu*, indirectly giving his cousin access to the splendours and extravagance of Diaghilev's ballets.

Fortuny was just eighteen when his mother decided to move to Venice, which was more affordable than Paris. She rented one floor of the Palazzo Martinengo, in the Cannaregio – the young Fortuny was immediately enthralled.

Equipped with a sophisticated camera and a Dubroni stereograph, Fortuny began to pace the city's alleyways, loving them as passionately and tenderly as his father had the sand dunes of Morocco. He began by capturing facets of daily life and architectural details of his adoptive city – the thousands of negatives would later prove to be sources of inspiration when he launched into dress design. It was perhaps Venice's dreamy atmosphere that influenced him the most. He never tired of the lagoon, the faded colours of the palazzos, their elegant décor, the arched, cat-like shape of the bridges, the ancient, oriental atmosphere of the city; or of the work of Venetian Renaissance painters such as Bellini, Titian and Veronese, and the hazy golden light immortalized by Giorgione.

When Fortuny left home, he took a modest attic floor in the city's largest Gothic palazzo. Some time later he was delighted to be able to move into the entire three thousand square metres of the Palazzo Orfei, and in 1905 he acquired the freehold. The city was quick to accept him – Venetians were irresistibly drawn to his inquiring and eccentric personality. He always spoke Venetian better than Italian, but he remained resolutely Spanish and keeping his original nationality was very important to him – Balenciaga later acknowledged that he had been Spain's greatest couturier of the day.

a t the turn of the century, Venice, rather than Vienna, Paris or Rome, was the cosmopolitan capital of Europe. People's habits and customs were interchangeable, and everyone knew everyone else. But Fortuny never really felt at home in society – he turned his palazzo into an enormous studio, a quiet retreat overlooking the lagoon. If he went to balls or the opera, travelled to Paris or Rome, or attended exhibitions in London or Berlin, he allowed his mood alone to dictate his choice of companions.

Fortuny's own artistic curiosity would undoubtedly sooner or later have led him to experiment with fashion, but he was certainly influenced by Henriette Négrin whom he met in Paris in about 1895. She was an artist's model, and was both stunning and clever – tall, blonde, with big sparkling eyes and delicate features. Seven years later, on 14 July 1902, the day the

Campanile of St Mark's collapsed, Fortuny arrived with her in Venice. His mother and sister greatly disapproved of her, and obstinately refused to receive her for three reasons: she was French, divorced and brought bad luck. (After all, she had arrived on the day of the collapse of the Campanile.) Undaunted, Henriette settled into the palazzo, where she lived for forty-seven happy years with Mariano, eventually marrying him; and for another fifteen sad years as a widow.

t he Fortuny style was the result of a collaboration between two people in love – he designed for an ideal of femininity, embodied by the real woman he knew so well. Fortuny designed the clothes and some of their decorative details, invented the pleated look and the dyeing processes and took out patents in his name only (eighteen in all in Paris, with similar ones all over Europe), but it was Henriette who, with an even surer touch, picked out the patterns and motifs from their Venetian surroundings and from the books in their extensive library that they adapted for their clothes. She often block-printed the patterns on the dresses, coats and capes herself, and most importantly, she supervised the production of the famous Fortuny pleated dresses. Because of her untiring efforts hundreds of 'Delphos' dresses made their 'society début' through the imposing doors of the palazzo.

Fortuny and Henriette were receptive and inquisitive designers. His detractors claimed he had an unprincipled lack of commitment and organization, but it would be fairer to describe him as having an encyclopaedic mind (amply justified by the variety of sources that inspired his hundreds of dress designs). He readily identified with the thirst for knowledge that characterized the sixteenth and eighteenth centuries, returning constantly to these sumptuous periods as an inspiration for his designs.

at the beginning of the twentieth century, fashion hesitated, marking time before either opting for the modernism of designers such as Jean Patou, Jeanne Lanvin or Madeleine Vionnet, or following the less adventurous path of a designer like Jacques Doucet. The century started on a backward-looking note, and fashion did too; it veered between a candy-coloured *style directoire* and the orientalism of the bazaar, from musk-scented India to the perfections of classicism, making a rapid detour via a medieval period crossed with exoticism: fashion was undergoing a hectic process of renewal. In such a context, Fortuny was never really a couturier; he did not present an annual collection, or show separate summer and winter designs. His aim was quite different – rather like the English Romantic painters before him, such as Sir Lawrence Alma-Tadema, John William Waterhouse, John Frederick Lewis or Albert Joseph Moore – he set out to find his own version of a timeless ideal form. It was a subtle blend of the Antique, the Orient and the Renaissance, which once finalized never changed. From then on he worked only on the technical aspects, continually improving and refining the dyeing processes, the quality of his fabrics and the pleated dresses.

It would be more accurate to talk of the Fortuny 'style' rather than of high fashion: from the point of view of conventional couture, the simplicity of his designs was astonishing for the period.

They were cut out flat in one piece, and although they might be superficially modern or Japanese in character — kimonos are traditionally stored flat — their finished shape betrayed the designer's limited skill as a cutter: Fortuny was not Vionnet. Only the overall effect mattered to him, so he always kept his distance from new forms and the details of the cut, which meant he was also detached from the dramas of mainstream fashion.

the 'Delphos' dress, with its many versions, stands out as the design most typical of the Fortuny style. It was named after the antique sculpture that inspired it, the 'Delphi Charioteer', a figure in a long chiton held in place at the shoulders by simple bronze clasps. The pleating of the material for these dresses was achieved by a process of evaporation: the wet and folded silk was laid on heated porcelain tubes, permanently fixing such tight pleats in the material so that the dresses looked carved, or pressed. The effect was that they elongated the women who wore them, just like Murano craftsmen draw out their molten glass. They effectively pared down the idealized 'flower-woman', so much a part of the previous period, until all that was left was her long and willowy stem; worn belted, they evoked for D'Annunzio pliant, gleaming sheaves of reeds.

fortuny used a vast range of sumptuous velvets, coats, jackets, kimonos, capes, shoes, hats, handbags and other accessories to complement the elegant dresses. The velvets as well as the silks were imported from Japan — their opulence counterbalanced the studied simplicity of the pleated dresses, setting off the fresh and unusual colours of the 'Delphos' with their gold, silver and bronze. However, Fortuny made a point of using lightweight velvets to create the effect he wanted – these clothes were to be worn by modern women, so it was just as important that they should be comfortable to wear as that they should recall their heavier Renaissance models; Fortuny reproduced their effect using cloth of unsurpassed delicacy and lightness, and retained their beauty, brilliance, elegance and richness.

Fortuny's velvets gave his clothes a theatrical flavour, using unusually generous amounts of material; stoles became all-enveloping, while full-length coats spread out in luxurious soft folds. Just as the 'Delphos' dresses were directly inspired by ancient Greece (which, reinterpreted through Fortuny's eyes, also had a hint of a draped Egyptian style and neo-classical, English romantic simplicity), the velvets too drew on every available historical source for ideal representations of beautiful clothing.

ortuny looked to Japan and the Venetian Renaissance – particularly the work of Carpaccio – for the definitive shape of his velvet clothes, but was more eclectic in his choice of motifs for their decoration. He introduced a style that was both light and finely detailed; again his inspiration was sometimes Greek, with foliage studded with gold, or star-shapes, or Cycladic water-plant forms in muted colours. Sometimes it was Byzantine, with facing pairs of birds in purple or royal blue, symbols of death and resurrection (Proust described his fascination with this symbol in the letters he wrote to Maria de

Madrazo, Fortuny's aunt, while he was gathering material for *A la Recherche du temps perdu*). Sometimes the inspiration came from Japan, with cherry blossom, chrysanthemums, peonies, and a particular Japanese colour, *wabi*, a mixture of a jade green wash and a coppery bronze; and again and again he returned to the Renaissance, with its abundance of foliage, damask patterns, vermilion pomegranates, rosy pineapples and greenish thistle shapes. He borrowed narrow gold- and silver-threaded borders from Indian saris and occasionally used strange primeval motifs in washed-out colours from Oceania and Africa; there were motifs from the Upper Nile in a harsh blue, rust, green or dark red. He turned to the East for inspiration, as his father had, and reinterpreted its indigo mosaics, filigree, delicately interlaced wrought-iron and damascening in his decoration. Seventeenth-century Spain suggested damasked velvet, though he was careful to soften and blend the rather sharp colours of the originals. Lastly, he took motifs from seventeenth- and eighteenth-century France, adapting the rustic, pastoral or exotic styles, using either a damasked background, or some floral and beaded details – rarely using both at once, in contrast with Paul Poiret.

f ortuny could be described as a couturier who worked from memory – his imagination drew on his experiences and his artistic apprenticeship, and he mixed his colours like a painter. He was a master of the art of merging and concealing his sources, giving each of his designs a unique and original character. He fired the imagination of some of the greatest creative artists of the period; for instance, Orson Welles used three of his coats in 1949 (the year of the artist's death) for the filming of *Othello*.

Though Fortuny's thoroughly romantic style, with its pleating and velvet, was closely linked to Venetian painting, he belonged more to the literary than the fashion world; he had a great interest in books, and many of his friends were writers. His creations lent themselves so well to being used in fiction that they quickly became props in significant books of the period.

Henri de Régnier featured his young friend Fortuny as a character in his novel *Altana*, and Paul Morand based his Zuliano Trevisan, the painter in *Les Extravagants*, on him, but Marcel Proust, Gabriele D'Annunzio, L. P. Hartley, and even Mary McCarthy limited themselves to using just his clothes in their narratives. (Hartley mentions them when his hero Eustace visits Venice, in his trilogy *Eustace and Hilda*; in McCarthy's *The Group* a dead woman is dressed in a Fortuny gown.) Both D'Annunzio and Proust recognized the impact of Fortuny the couturier, giving his creations a significant role in their books.

In 1894 D'Annunzio moved into Prince Hohenlohe's famous Casetta Rossa, near the Fortuny family home at Palazzo Martinengo, and from then on, he and Fortuny saw a great deal of each other. The two young men worked together from the end of 1898 on the play *Francesca da Rimini*, casting Eleanora Duse in the title role, with costumes designed by Fortuny. The project failed, however, because the writer and his muse had been expecting Fortuny to finance the scheme. Later joint efforts were no more successful, but the literary possibilities of Fortuny's work had made a big impression on D'Annunzio, and in his novel *Forse che si, forse che no* he dressed his Isabella in Fortuny clothes. The night scene on the terrace overlooking the Tyrrhenian Sea, in which the young woman dances for her lover while slowly unfastening her 'Delphos' dress, stands out as one of the most tender and sensual ever written by D'Annunzio. It is full of foreboding of both the anxiety and moral vulnerability of the heroine, who, overcome by misery, later abandons one of her dresses in her flight; it is left hanging on the end of her bed, a pathetic sloughed skin – a symbol and prophecy of her twilight's madness.

Proust passed an equally harsh judgment on Fortuny – Oriane de Guermantes receives the narrator wrapped in a Fortuny kimono-type dressing gown, the colour of a butterfly's wing, and certainly looks very beautiful. But she is unlucky in love, and he does not find her desirable; the narrator pointedly refers to the unpleasant smell of her dress (caused by the Chinese crystallized egg white used as a fixative by Fortuny). Even more than D'Annunzio's Isabella, an occasional rebel, Proust's Albertine is a passive and phlegmatic victim, wearing clothes of her jailer's choosing. Her Fortuny dressing gowns 'à la Guermantes' show her off, but crush her too; they fuel the fantasies of the narrator and make the wearer more accessible to his desires. Proust used the Fortuny clothes as symbols, sinister outward signs of the sado-masochistic relationship of the narrator and Albertine.

1 iterature passed a heavy sentence on Fortuny, but his clients, by contrast, found much to celebrate in his style; the sensual curves and ease of his clothes rejected modernism, challenging the stripes and right angles favoured by Art Deco.

The pleated silks immediately struck a chord with Isadora Duncan, and she went to Venice specially to buy a 'Delphos' for herself and to have another made to order for her daughter Deirdre. She was followed by Eleanora Duse and the Grammatica sisters, all D'Annunzio's beautiful friends, even the eccentric marquise Casati.

Fortuny boutiques were opened in every city then considered chic: Paris, Vienna, London, New York, and so society women began to try on the clothes, but with less success – this dignified and voluptuous, monumental and intimate style suited the less respectable women of the 'demi-monde' better than any others. Among Fortuny's clients were the 'three graces' of the profession: Cléo de Mérode, Liane de Pougy and Emilienne d'Alençon, who were 'role models' of femininity, fashion and sophistication.

t he immediate success of Fortuny's creations (from 1910 until the forties) was largely owing to his encapsulation of a Venetian collective memory – the essence of the Sérénissima came through both in the soft folds of velvet and the sophistication of a 'Delphos'. It was thanks to Fortuny's intensive detailed research that each of his dresses carried with it the indescribable flavour of Venice; he achieved a personal style using a huge variety of influences, at the same time creating a style that was truly Venetian. Fortuny realized his ideal so completely in the realm of fashion that together he and Henriette were able to maintain the popularity of his designs for forty-five years. The mingled Eastern and Renaissance influences on their clothes were also an integral part of the grand and varied setting of their lives and work.

Fortuny had a passion for Wagner, and he deliberately applied the Germanic principles of *Gesammtkunstwerk* to his own life. According to these, art must be absolute, touching all aspects of life. Fortuny's *Gesammtkunstwerk* was embodied in the Palazzo Orfei (later renamed Palazzo Fortuny) which its creator filled with his personality, in the same way as Des Esseintes in *A Rebours* by Huysmans, and as advocated by Edgar Allan Poe in his treatise on decoration.

It was as if Wagner's phantom ship, 'The Flying Dutchman', had come to rest in the Campo San Benedetto, and its captain, after emptying his trunks and spreading out the riches collected on his travels, had decided to stop roaming the seas to devote himself to the arts.

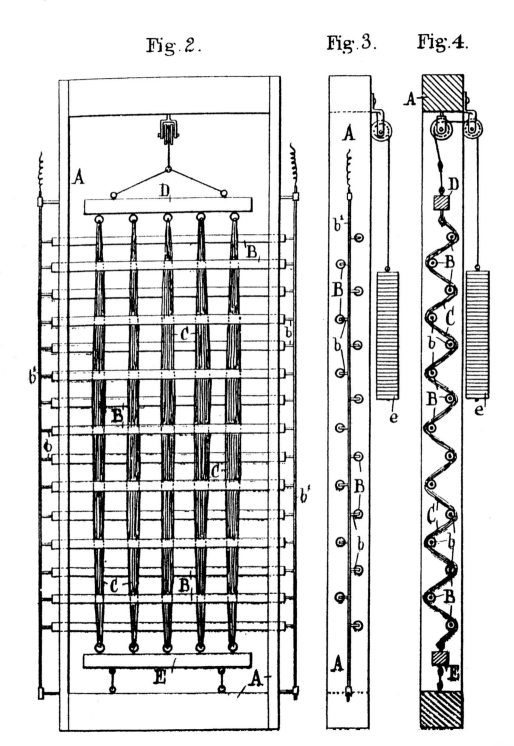

Fig. 2.

Fig. 3.

Fig. 4.

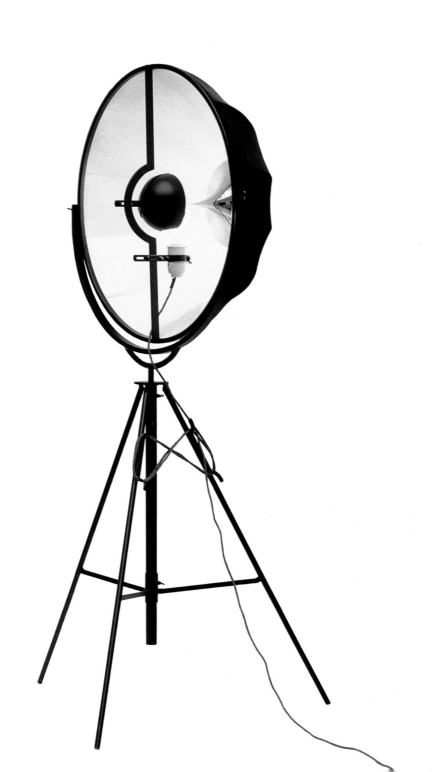

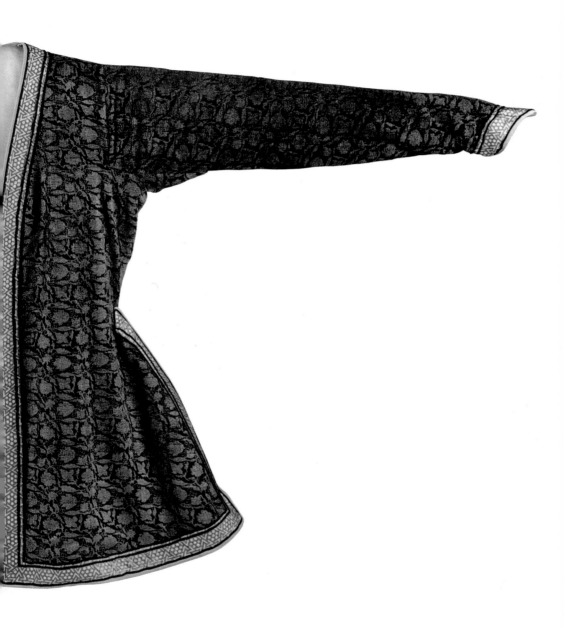

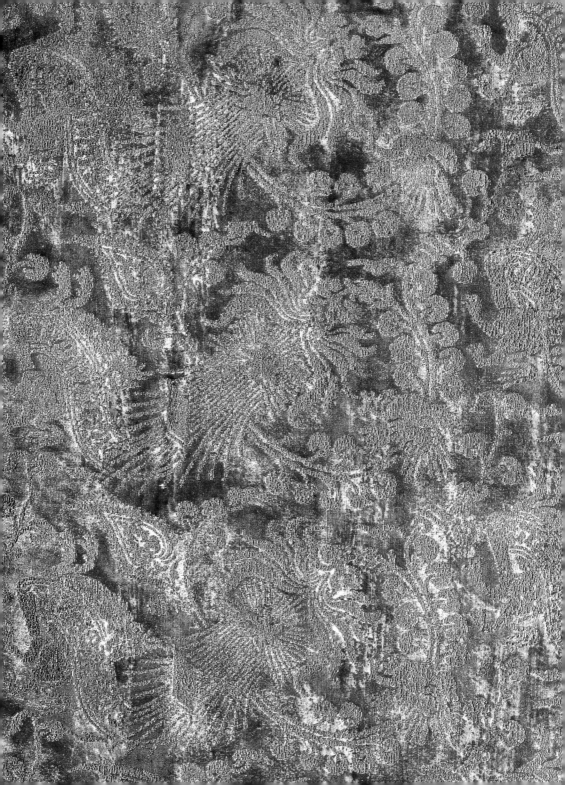

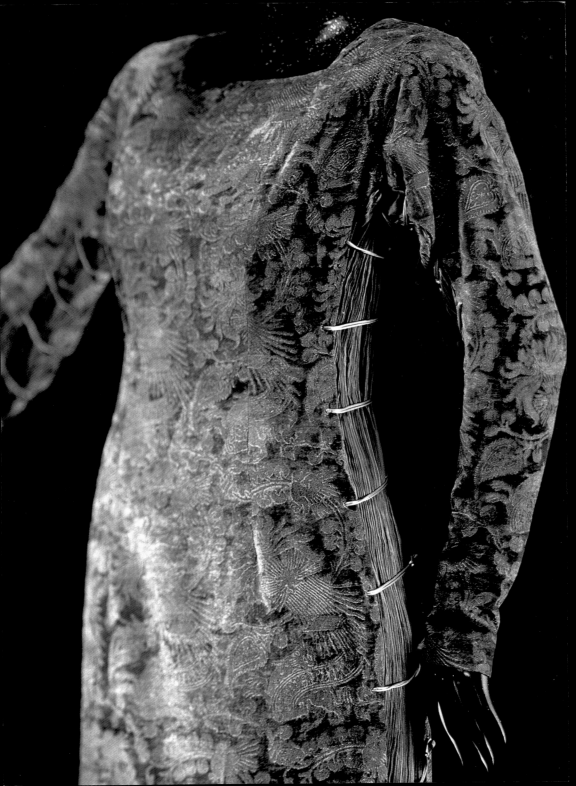

Chronology

1871   Born in Granada on 11 May, the son of Mariano Fortuny y Marsal and Cecilia de Madrazo.

1874   Death of Mariano Fortuny y Marsal on 21 November in Rome.

1875   Leaves Italy for France, Rome for Paris.

1889   Leaves Paris for Venice. His family occupies one floor of the Palazzo Martinengo in the Cannaregio. Studies art at the Accademia.

1892   Goes to Bayreuth, where he discovers Wagner and theatre design. His interest in innovative theatre leads first to set design, and then fashion.

1897   Awarded the gold medal at the Munich International Festival of Art for his painting *The Flower-girls*, a work influenced by Wagner's ideas. From then on he exhibits at every Venice Biennale until his death.

1902   Henriette Négrin, whom he met in Paris, comes to live with him in Venice. They get married much later, and remain together until his death.

1905   Acquires the freehold of Palazzo Orfei, later renamed Palazzo Fortuny.

1907   Experiments theoretically with textiles for the first time, according to his records.

1909   Opens the first Fortuny boutique in the palazzo.

1912   Shows his textiles in the Spanish pavilion at the International Exhibition of Decorative Arts in Paris. He is by now a well-known designer, although unconventional.

1919   Giancarlo Stucky, owner of the Mulini Stucky in Venice, and Fortuny's friend and patron, decides to establish the Fabbrica Fortuny (Fabbrica di Tessuti Artistici Fortuny) on the Giudecca. Fortuny's Spanish

Medieval-style dress in blue silk velvet, printed with Byzantine motifs. The panels of pleated silk satin in a matching colour are linked to the velvet of the dress by loops of braid, finished with Murano glass beads. © Kyoto Costume Institute, photo Minsei Tominaga.

nationality precludes him from owning a factory on Italian soil, so he is given the official title of artistic director. The studios are equipped with machinery made to his own specifications, still in use today.

1933 After financial and accounting problems, the Fabbrica is sold; with Fortuny's agreement it passes from Stucky to Elsie McNeill Lee, later contessa Gozzi, a young American designer who worked regularly with Fortuny. She turns the business round and makes it an international success.

1936, Inherits his father's collections on the deaths of his mother and his
1938 sister and arranges them in Palazzo Orfei, giving it an oriental flavour. Palazzo Martinengo is abandoned.

1938 Makes a remarkable journey with Henriette across Africa as far as Sudan. Sketches daily, in honour of his father. On their return, they find Fascist Italy has cut itself off from the world. Imports of silk and velvet are suspended. After unsuccessful attempts with mediocre Italian fabrics, he falls back on his stocks of Japanese silk, which are quickly used up. He is obliged to stop work altogether.

1949 Dies on 2 May at Palazzo Orfei. The Fortuny couture studios are closed for good; the boutique in the palazzo remains open until the death of Henriette, even though there are fewer and fewer clients. The Fabbrica remains; production of the cotton fabrics, suspended during the war, is resumed and continues to this day.

1965 Death of Henriette Fortuny in Venice.

A simply cut medieval-style dress. The dark silk velvet is embellished on the deep hem and on the bodice with intricate gold oriental arabesques. Painted background, and Fortuny cushions. © Fortuny Museum, Venice.

Fortuny

Figure of Queen Nefertiti clothed in thin pleated linen (c. 1365–1349 BC, red quartzite, height: 29 cm). Fortuny's dress designs were inspired by the effect of this pleating. Musée du Louvre, Paris. © Editions Assouline.
The actress Natasha Rambova, one of Rudolph Valentino's wives, wearing a 'Delphos'. This contemporary photograph by James Abbe captures the innovative impact of such dresses. © Kathryn Abbe Photographs, Glen Head, New York.

A rich miscellany of 'Delphos' dresses. The shoulders and seams were accentuated by glass beads, made specially for Fortuny by Murano craftsmen. Black and gold dress: gift of Elizabeth Sweeting, originally worn by Eleanora Duse; blue dress: gift of Miss Elilie Gigsby; apricot dress: gift of Miss Irene Worth. © The Victoria and Albert Museum, London, photo R. I. Davis.

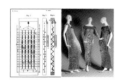

'The Infernal Machine', patented by Fortuny, was used to make the pleats in the silk satin used for the 'Delphos' dresses. Patent no. 414.119, 10 June 1909, describes it as for 'a type of wavy pleated material'. © Institut national de la propriété industrielle, Paris.
Three 'Delphos' dresses in pleated silk satin. © The Metropolitan Museum of Art, New York.

Three of the adoptive daughters of Isadora Duncan, the American dancer. From left to right: Lisa (the most well known), Anna and Margot. These dresses used to be wrongly attributed to Paul Poiret, who sold Fortuny 'Delphos' dresses in his shop, Rosine. © Roger-Viollet, Harlingue-Viollet collection, Paris.
Evening cape in silk velvet with gold printed decoration, worn over a 'Delphos' (gift of G. J. Vincent Minetti, 1972). © The Metropolitan Museum of Art, New York.

Coloured samples of the silk satins used for the 'Delphos' dresses, preserved by Elsie McNeill Lee, contessa Gozzi, who took over the Fortuny business after Fortuny died in 1949. Elsie Lee Gozzi collection, Venice. © All Rights Reserved.

Illustration from *Vogue* (Paris, 1924). Medieval-style dress of silk velvet with pleated silk panels inserted at the sides, and a short evening coat in garnet-red silk velvet, printed with gold oriental motifs. © Condé Nast Publications Ltd.
Portrait of the actress Lilian Gish in a 'Delphos' dress in pleated silk satin. In the twenties, Hollywood and many of its actresses fell in love with the Fortuny style. © Photo Nell Dorr.

Medieval dress in gold silk velvet, with the freely adapted Renaissance motif of the thistle-flower and its leaves. The straight panels of pleated silk are kept in place by loops of braid, finished with glass beads of a matching colour. © Kyoto Costume Institute, photo Minsei Tominaga.

The 'primo piano nobile' (first reception hall) in the Palazzo Orfei, photographed by Fortuny. His fabrics, collections and paintings can be seen, with the diffused lighting he was so fond of using. © Centro di documentazione di Palazzo Fortuny.

Portrait of Henriette Fortuny. Engraving. © National Library, Madrid. **Rare example of the use of plain silk in Fortuny's work.** An oriental coat in deep pink with gold printed pattern, with wide slashed sleeves, round collar, and all the edges embellished with braid and glass beads from Murano (gift of Mr Courtland Palmer, 1950). © The Metropolitan Museum of Art, New York.

Mariano Fortuny in his library, one of the most appealing portraits of the artist, showing him absorbed in his work. His library table was a splendid antique, more like a table for a sumptuous banquet than a desk. © Fortuny Museum, Venice.

A 'Delphos' dress in pleated silk satin, with a romantic-style high waist. In this photo, Fortuny particularly wanted to show the unusual length of his dresses, and how they emphasized his models' figures. In the background is a screen covered in Fortuny silk velvet, printed with a Flemish and French Renaissance-style pomegranate pattern. © Fortuny Museum, Venice.

Two Fortuny lamps, reissued by Andrée Putman for Ecart International and in production since the early eighties. Fortuny had an Art Deco style lamp on his own desk; he invented the spot-light to use in studio shots of his models. Museums have adopted similar lighting systems – they are very effectively used at the Scuola di San Rocco in Venice to light Tintoretto's series of paintings. © Ecart International, photo Deidi von Schaewen.

Two magnificent panoramas by Fortuny, showing how breadth of style was also a feature of his photography. The first, capturing a luxurious tourist's image, is reminiscent of the paintings of John Singer Sargent; the second is a darker and more mysterious scene, in spite of the presence of the little girl on the left. © Fortuny Museum, Venice.

A 'Delphos' dress with 'wave pleats', invented by Fortuny around 1915, and imitated today by Issey Miyake. Illustration Anne Cluzel. © Editions Assouline. **Isadora Duncan and her Russian husband**, the poet Sergei Essenin, with one of her adoptive daughters, Irma Duncan, wearing a 'Delphos' ensemble: a sleeveless dress and tunic, both in pleated silk satin and edged with Murano glass beads. © Roger-Viollet, Harlingue-Viollet collection, Paris.

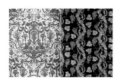

Length of cloth (3.48 x 1.26 m) with pattern based on eighteenth-century French designs, produced by Fortuny for his private collection (gift of Miss Jeanette Young). © The Art Institute of Chicago.
Black silk velvet with vine-branch pattern printed in gold, a motif used by Fortuny for liturgical decorations. © The Victoria and Albert Museum, London.

Two coloured autochrome prints, showing medieval and Renaissance styles in silk velvet, printed with patterns in gold and silver. In the background, panels covered with Fortuny material – one a rich purple silk velvet, the other a silk painted with intricate leaf patterns. Fortuny cushions on the floor. © Fortuny Museum, Venice.

Fortuny himself arranged this tableau to show his first design, a simple rectangle of cotton, later of silk, printed with Cycladic motifs in pale colours, and called 'Knossos'. © Fortuny Museum, Venice.

One of the few kimonos made by Fortuny, of silk satin in the Japanese moiré colour, *wabi*. It is hand painted with the cherry-tree motif – an oriental 'memento mori'. © Private collection.
Fortuny as engraver: a woman's shoe, probably from the Correr Museum, Venice, or the Cluny Museum, Paris, both of which he haunted to find inspiration for his own collections. © National Library, Madrid.

Photograph by Fortuny, showing the 'primo piano nobile' (first reception hall) in the Palazzo Orfei. Fortuny used this huge hall as, among other things, his showroom. © Fortuny Museum, Venice.

'Delphos' dress in pleated silk satin and jacket in silk voile, edged with Murano beads; photographed by Fortuny in the palazzo. © Fortuny Museum, Venice.
Evening coat in blue silk velvet with silver printed decoration, and pale pink 'Delphos' dress in pleated silk satin. 'Fashion in art, the century's forms and colours', Messieurs Millon and Robert, Drouot-Montaigne, 29 November 1994. © Bernard Richebé.

The 'Knossos' rectangles shown by Fortuny's models in a pastoral tableau typical of fashion shows at the time, in which a theme was invented for each collection; a technique recently enjoying a revival with Jean-Paul Gaultier and John Galliano. © Fortuny Museum, Venice.

Three Fortuny dresses. From left to right: brownish pink silk velvet printed with gold (gift of Mrs Henry T. Ashmore, 1970); grey-blue silk crêpe printed with gold (gift of Mrs Leonard Smiley, 1975); indoor dress in gold silk velvet (gift of Miss Emily Chase, 1948). © The Metropolitan Museum of Art, New York.
Detail of a piece of purple velvet, printed with silver motifs. © The Victoria and Albert Museum, London, photo Sara Hodges.

Woman's jacket in silk velvet, printed with a mosaic of intricate oriental motifs in gold and silver, and edged with a ribbon printed with hearts, six-pointed stars and spots (modern lining). © The Los Angeles County Museum of Art.

Detail of a woman's jacket, silk velvet printed with gold, raw silk printed with minute patterns, and edged with Murano glass beads. © The Los Angeles County Museum of Art.
Evening coat in ivory silk with block-printed patterns. The silk panels are linked by Murano glass beads. 'La Mode dans l'Art', 1890–1990, Messieurs Millon and Robert, Drouot-Montaigne, 5 June 1991. © All Rights Reserved.

Two black-and-white photographs by Fortuny. He posed his models in the studio at his palazzo; one wears his famous 'Delphos' dress, and the other, a medieval dress in silk velvet with inserted side panels of pleated silk satin. The two styles are set off by day capes in printed silk voile, fastened with braid loops decorated with Murano glass beads. © Fortuny Museum, Venice.

Detail of a piece of cloth in purple silk velvet, printed with intricate silver arabesques, half Renaissance, half oriental. © The Victoria and Albert Museum, London, photo Sara Hodges.
Black 'Delphos' dress in pleated silk satin with an oriental jacket in silk velvet with gold printed pattern (modern lining). © The Victoria and Albert Museum, London.

Portrait of Selma Schubert by her brother the photographer Alfred Stieglitz, wearing an orange-coloured 'Delphos' dress with matching flowers on the belt, under a cardigan (gift of Georgia O'Keeffe, 1955). © The Metropolitan Museum of Art, New York.

Acknowledgments

The publishers would like to thank Silvio Fuso, curator at the Fortuny Museum, Venice, and also Minsei Tominaga, Deidi von Schaewen, Bernard Richebé, Kathryn Abbe (Kathryn Abbe Photographs, Glen Head, New York), Haydn Hansell (the Victoria and Albert Picture Library, London), Sara Hodges (photographer for the Victoria and Albert Museum), Micheline Monka (Institut national de la propriété industrielle, Paris), Deirdre Donohue (The Metropolitan Museum of Art, New York), Rye Nii (The Kyoto Costume Institute, Kyoto), Michel Taural (Ecart International, Paris), Luisa Cuenca (National Library, Madrid), Françoise Auguet (expert for Messieurs Millon and Robert, Paris), Dominique Georget (student with Messieurs Millon and Robert, Paris), Kimberly D. Costas (The Los Angeles County Museum, Los Angeles), Atalanta Bouboulis (former director of the Fabbrica Fortuny, Venice), Adrienne Jeske (The Art Institute of Chicago, Chicago) and Condé Nast Publications.